The Little Red Handbook

Of

Public Speaking

and

Presenting

STEPHEN KEAGUE

DEDICATION

To my ever supportive MC. Darling, you are my rock. Without your dedication and support, so little in my life would be possible. Last but not least, to my two girls, who I am sure among other things, can use this as a reference for future acceptance speeches....

CONTENTS

ACKNOWLEDGMENTS

I would like to thank all those people who helped either directly or indirectly in my own personal development and perhaps unknowingly the development and creation of this book. It has been a long journey and many people have contributed in one way or another, those who have touched my life and those where merely paths have crossed. Learning from observation and immersion, a valuable source of knowledge is experience. This book is a compilation of "notes to self", based upon my own personal experience of presenting and speaking in public – from business conferences to weddings.

1 OVERVIEW

Yes! The number one phobia that most people share is making a presentation; speaking in front of a group of other people: colleagues, strangers, it doesn't seem to matter - it's scary. Having to make a speech or presenting in front of a group can be nerve wracking, no matter how small or familiar the group may be. There is no doubt that it involves a level of confidence and a lot of preparation.

If you are making your first speech or presentation, or if you need to make your presentations or speeches more engaging, more powerful, more structured, more interesting, more persuasive and more concise (whilst at the same time need to make it less fearful for you), then this book will help deliver everything you need.

It will give you the skills, knowledge and tools to plan, design and deliver effective, memorable presentations and speeches. It will enable you to make fearless presentations and speeches in the future and have the confidence of knowing that you have the audience on your side.

Become a great presenter and excel at public speaking. This book will show you what you need to know. We all have the power to deliver memorable presentations and speeches. With a little work, you too can find the power.

This book is based upon both my own experiences and observations. I have purposely kept it concise to deliver the key information quickly and also so it may be used as a continuous reference. A handbook in the preparation of current, more immediate, or future presentations and speeches.

This book can be used again and again as a reference in the preparation and structure for all of your presentation and speech needs.

This book will focus on the three P's of presentation skills: Plan, Purpose and Performance. These three components combine seamlessly, for successful presentations and speeches:

Plan:

Planning ahead for the event and positioning yourself to take advantage of all possible opportunities, and to overcome any of the potential problems. The old adage is as true now as it has always been 'Failing to prepare is preparing to fail'

Purpose:

What is the purpose of the presentation? What do you want to cover? What is the message, the content of your presentation and how it is structured?

Performance:

Develop your verbal and nonverbal communication skills, communicating effectively, getting the message across. Remember the three E's: Energy, Enthusiasm and Excitement. It is catching, if you don't have them, no one else will.

2 PLAN

Preparing for a Presentation or Speech. Proper Planning and Preparation Prevents Poor Performance.

Questions to ask in advance

The questions you ask in advance will determine how well you have planned for your success and the successful delivery of your presentation or speech. Planning is critical to ensure your presentation or speech is focused correctly. Some problems that can arise when making a presentation or speech are often related to the event, presentation content, your message, the venue and the audience. The more information you can get, the better prepared you will be.

Whenever you are asked to speak, you should have a list of questions, some or all of which may be applicable, on the following:

The Event

- What is the overall purpose of the event?
- What, day, date, time and place?
- What is your role in the event?
- Who are the other speakers and their topics?
- Who introduces you? Provide a self-composed, brief introduction if necessary.
- What is your order of appearance?
- What is the agenda?
- Will it be recorded, or will there be press coverage?
- Are there special considerations, such as politics, language, culture, ethics?
- What is the dress code/appropriate dress?

The Presentation/Message

- What are your objectives? What is the purpose of your presentation? What message do you want to deliver?

- What do you want to cover? What do you want to achieve in your presentation or speech?

- How long is the presentation? How long do you have to speak? Never exceed sixty minutes without giving the audience a break.

- Will there be time for questions? How much? When?

- What examples can you use that will make your presentation or message clearer to the audience?

The Venue

- Where is the room in which you speak?

- When can you have access to the room?

- How large is it?

- What time can you set up?

- What is the seating arrangement?

- Where do you enter and exit?

- Where do you speak?

- Will they provide the equipment you need, or should you take your own?

- Do you have a lectern/microphone/audio visual equipment?

- Where do you put your notes and or other equipment?

The Audience

- How many people will attend?

- What are their backgrounds?

- How familiar are they with the subject?

- Will there be language difficulties? Primary language? Interpreters?

Set-up properly on the day

On the day of your presentation, take time to make sure you're organised and mentally prepared for what lies ahead. Allow plenty of time for travel to the venue, planning to arrive at least an hour before you are due to speak. Before you leave for the venue, make sure you have back-up copies of your presentation material, so you know your material is safe if you experience any technical problems with equipment.

When you get there, check that you are happy with the layout of the room and that all the equipment you need is there. Make sure that you spend time in the room before your presentation or speech, get to know the room and run through your material beforehand to ensure that everything is in order and working smoothly.

Make sure the room you will be using is well-illuminated. Poor lighting in a room will affect the internal clock of your audience. This may cause them to tune out on you and your message and worse case, perhaps even fall asleep!

Do not use any presentation tool that may require you to dim the lights completely. If the room has windows, tilt the blinds to obstruct the view. You do not want anyone looking out the windows and daydreaming during your presentation or speech, or people looking in the windows and distracting the audience.

Keep all noise during your presentation to an absolute minimum. Unplug all phones in the room and turn off any overhead speakers and mobile phones. Understandably some of your audience may need to remain contactable, but at a minimum request that mobile phones are set to silent or vibrate. If an attendee does need to take a call please request that they leave the room prior to answering their phone. If the room you will be using has adjacent facilities, make sure an event won't be taking place, which could cause disruption during your presentation.

Remove all possible distractions

Get rid of clutter, boxes, piles of papers and anything else that is not directly related to your presentation. Remove any possible distractions. When you have the attention of the audience, you want to keep it.

Arrange for refreshments

No need to go overboard here, but make sure at a minimum you have on hand, bottled water. I have attended events where they have often over-catered on refreshments, with large assortments of beverages and snacks to choose from. The audience have not come to your presentation or speech to eat, they have come to listen. This can be a distraction, again taking away the attention of the audience.

Handouts

You have gone to a lot of effort to produce your presentation or speech. Although understandably you may not have handouts associated with a speech, leaving handouts for a presentation will reinforce your message, and will help the audience to remember your presentation when they look at them again. It gives the audience even more value from attending your presentation. Always include your contact details so that the audience can contact you. But leave the handouts until the end of your presentation because these should be a take away and not a distraction during your actual presentation. Don't compete with your own material. If possible, arrange for each attendee to have a pen or pencil and paper provided with the seating for note-taking.

3 PURPOSE

What is the purpose of the presentation or speech? What do you want to cover? What is the message, the content of your presentation and how it is structured? It is all in the VOICE. This is an easy way to remember the following elements and structure of a successful presentation or speech:

Vision – First, establish your vision, the theme for the audience and your Objectives

Opening - Common ground, interests, experiences, link to the previous speaker

Introduction - Purpose and Topics, Agenda

Content -This is the main body or the message of the presentation

Ending - Summary, Questions and Closing

Vision

Take a good look at understanding your audience and your objectives. This should be based upon the questions you ask in advance of any presentation or speech, (refer to Chapter 2 for a list of useful questions). Whenever you are asked to speak, you should have a list of questions. Ask yourself: What information do you have? What do people want from the presentation or speech? What will interest them? What affects them?

Other presenters or colleagues may provide ideas for your presentation or speech too. You certainly don't want to repeat other speakers, but you should relate your presentation to theirs.

Choose a topic that you feel comfortable with. Look through old speeches or colleagues presentations, as these can give you ideas. Give yourself enough time. If possible, to play with different themes and gain feedback from potential audience members or colleagues.

If someone else has chosen the topic, one which you may be less than enthusiastic, try to focus on the positive points, the ones you most like.

Opening

Find a common ground, interests, experiences, link to the previous speaker. Make sure you come across as sincere and interested. Wherever possible give personal illustrations. Ask a question: ask the audience a relevant question they have probably never asked themselves, but now that they have heard it they will really want to know the answer. Only reveal the answer at the end of the presentation or speech. Say something unexpected. Speak what is on their mind. Use a few words of their language or make a surprising statement, example or statistic. This is like an informal ice breaker or attention grabber before the introduction.

Introduction

With the introduction identify your purpose, presentation or speech topic and agenda, your 'Roadmap' as such. Show the value: that your presentation or speech has something to offer, something in it for them - make them want to hear more.

Content

This is the main body or the message of the presentation. This should be divided into three topics, most relevant to your message. People tend to remember lists of three things. The audience are likely to remember only three things from your presentation.

Structure your presentation around threes and it will become more memorable.

The Rule of Three – We remember three things. Use Chronological, Developmental or Impact progression to develop your speech, for example:

- **Chronological**

  Sequence of information is historical.

  History – Current – Future

- **Developmental**

  Topics develop one after the other and require ensuring that each topic is understood before proceeding to the next one. Take questions between topics.

- **Impact**

  The sequence of information can have great impact on understanding and persuasion. Normally, a speaker introduces topics that the audience will agree with first, slowly proceeding to the controversial issues (the path of least resistance/ Good News-Bad News) leaving them last. Sometimes if the speaker knows the controversy is on the minds of the audience already, he or she is stronger, less defensive, for bringing up the controversy first. The introduction of bad news first can be high risk.

  While you can use examples that appeal to values, never argue them.

Try to use single words or short phrases for the topic titles. Make your message clear, concise and simple. Use examples and language that relates to the audience and is jargon free. Back up topics with examples, evidence, demonstrations. Use short sentences and simple words.

Be consistent and tie points to your overall theme.

Ending

Your purpose is to make your audience see what you saw, hear what you heard, feel what you felt. Give a summary, reinforce your key points, and leave no room for doubt about the important areas. Give them next steps, specific action or recommendations they can take away.

Take questions. Try this: "What questions do you have?" instead of "Are there any questions?". Count to ten, silently, to yourself after you ask any questions, this gives the audience a chance to raise a question. I have witnessed speakers who have closed with "Any questions? No? Thank you" all in the same breath; this is not professional and gives the impression that the speaker just can't get off the stage quick enough. Allow the time for questions; this is important and valuable interaction with your audience. Take note of any questions you were asked, as this is good material for your next presentation. If you take a question away to provide more information or contacts for a member of the audience, make sure you get their contact details and then do what you promised.

In closing, take your last chance to make a positive impression, end with a positive message, the most important point you want to make. Motivate them to do something, make them feel positive, inspired, challenged.

End with an upbeat finale, never end with a problem. Give an inspirational success story/quotation, "let me leave you with one important point".

Give the audience the answer to that relevant question they have probably never asked themselves, but now that they have heard it they will really want to know the answer - the one you may have posed during the opening.

4 PERFORMANCE

If your presentations or speeches are not well received, then there can be only one of two reasons. Either your approach is wrong or the message is wrong. By approach I mean how you present the information, your vocal intonation, body language and feelings towards presenting or public speaking.

There is an extremely important part of presentation skills, and this is practice. Without practice your Performance will be poor. I have known management and many executives with unrealistic expectations about their speaking ability, believing they can give a great presentation or speech without much effort. This attitude leads to significant frustration when their lax efforts fail to get the message across and fail to produce the desired results. Just because you may run a market leading company doesn't mean you can deliver a successful presentation with little or no effort, preparation or practice.

One of the biggest mistakes I see is where people believe they can "wing it", but in reality those who appear to be "winging it" are often very well practiced and prepared. 'Off-the-cuff' should mean well planned and practiced.

Once you accept the fact that making effective presentations and speeches is a learned skill, taking the time to practice is a natural step. Practice, practice and practice again.

Practice

Give yourself plenty of time. Don't leave it to the very last minute to practice your presentation or speech. When you know you have to present leave yourself real time to practice and this is more than just the night before. Plan at least eight hours for practice over the week before. I see no end of people who spend hours pouring over bullet points but fail to practice properly for the presentation.

Lack of practice is probably the most common mistake of all presentations or speeches that I have seen. The more familiar you become with your material, the more the words flow from you, credibly and passionately. The more comfortable you feel with your words, the more naturally you present your speech and deliver your message. Practice your presentation and it will get better. That is why good speakers practice – and practice again. I suggest that you should practice your presentation or speech out loud at least four times. I know you may suggest that you don't always have time, but please make time, I have seen many presentations let down due to lack of practice.

There are a number of ways for you to practice your presentation or speech:

In front of a mirror – Seeing yourself will improve your presentation. You will notice posture, gestures and mannerisms that you may never have noticed before. And you will begin to make changes

Audio – Listening to yourself is also a tool to use when you practice your presentation or speech. Immediately you will know if you are speaking too quickly, too slowly, or if some words are difficult to understand. You will hear mistakes in grammar and inappropriate "um's" and "ah's" that are easily removed from your presentation when you are aware of them. The audio sessions will also help to focus on content and vocal skills.

Video – Capture your presentation on film, nothing will improve your presentation more than seeing yourself. This will give you some immediate feedback and will enable you to fine-tune your performance. Video is a tool to use when you practice your presentation for both seeing and listening to yourself. It is the closest you will get to seeing your complete presentation or speech as your audience will.

Recording a presentation is the staple of many presentation training companies – so why not save time and money and do it yourself?

Practice in front of a really scary audience – family, friends, partners, colleagues, children. They will tell you quite plainly and honestly where you are going wrong, what you are doing well and provide the support that you need.

Practice against the clock – if you have to give a presentation or speech in a short period of time then try to practice against the clock. This is particularly true with something like the two to five minute presentation or speech, the "elevator pitch" (or elevator speech) used to quickly and simply deliver a message, define a product, service, or organization and its value proposition. The name "elevator pitch" reflects the idea that it should be possible to deliver a key message in the time span of an elevator ride. You can add to your script or remove items to fit the time allocated. Allow extra time in your presentation for questions and watch out for nerves as this could mean you talk faster on the day of your presentation or speech. On the day of the actual presentation or speech you could take in a clock, take off your wrist watch or have a timekeeper, MC (Master of Ceremonies) or Compère present so you stay on track with your timings.

Non-verbal Communication

Kinesics is the study of movement and nonverbal behavior. How we move, our posture and gestures are often related to how others perceive us our strengths or weaknesses. Certain movements can mean "open" or truthful, while others lead the observer to believe we are "closed" or defensive, or hiding something. In fact we may feel open minded, but our body language may suggest something entirely different than we would like.

Proxemics is the use of space. The way we use our space makes an impression on others as well.

Someone whose body language takes up very little space can be perceived as, weak or unimportant. Taking up too much space or invading someone else's space is not the answer either. "Horizontal" space is important for those who may be shorter or lack natural "vertical" space.

Be aware of how movement and the use of space can create a feeling of perceived personal confidence and credibility for others.

Non-verbal Behavior

Some studies show that the majority of our impressions of others are non-verbal. People believe more in how we make the statement or deliver a message in how we stand, look at them, and emphasize certain words than what we actually say. Television has changed the way we communicate; the messenger is just as important, maybe more so than the message itself. People must buy or accept us before they will the message.

What is the image you want to portray to your audience? What do they expect? Most of us want to see 'SOCCER' portray the following:

- **Sincerity**
- **Openness**
- **Credibility**
- **Confidence**
- **Enthusiasm**
- **Reliability**

But what do these look like? Perhaps it is easier to look at and understand the opposite of these traits; Insincere, Defensive, Lack of Credibility, Unconfident, Unenthusiastic and Unreliable.

We usually know what these traits look like, but unfortunately we don't realize how many times some of our non-verbal habits translate into negative messages to others.

Bad eye contact, slumped shoulders, poor posture, monotone, high pitched or too soft a voice, folded arms; all can be negative signals to an audience.

Most people tend to make quick judgments too, they usually decide within four minutes or less whether they like or trust the speaker. That means first impressions are extremely important. First impressions include your behavior even before you speak, as you wait to be introduced.

Generally, the best speakers use the following postures: their arms are open - outward gestures and hands are open or loosely clasped at waist, definitely not in pockets. Looking directly at as many people as possible, two to four second eye contact is best. Keeping head straight, neither tilted too high nor bowed. Weight should be balanced on both legs, shoulder width apart. Shoulders should be straight and relaxed not rigid.

Delivery

Remember, the way you approach the audience, the way you walk to the stage, the way you face them at the beginning can determine whether the audience will be attentive or not.

As you wait to be introduced:

- Breathe deeply.

- Don't appear disinterested in your own introduction or in other speaker's presentations, listen carefully to and look at the person who introduces you, occasionally looking at the audience.

- Remain seated if possible, for your introduction.

After your introduction:

- Walk confidently, but carefully to the lectern or place where you will be presenting.

- Don't rush.

- Establish eye contact with as many people as possible, "take in" your audience.

- Stop, pause for a few seconds, breathe deeply, smile, and allow yourself to relax for a moment. Only now should you begin to speak.

Delivery tips:

- Speak up.

- Vary your pace and voice levels.

- Sound enthusiastic.

- Pause occasionally.

- Use natural gestures, directing your movements towards the audience.

- Don't speak while you are facing away from your audience.

Gestures

Many of us gesture while we talk in normal conversations with others. Somehow, those natural gestures are often lost when we stand up to address a group. Since we want to look natural when we speak, gestures are perfectly appropriate. In addition, we reinforce the message by drawing visual pictures with our hands. Gestures should be tailored to the size of the space in which you are speaking. For example, you can use very broad gestures if you are addressing a very large group, but you would keep your hands closer to your body if the group is small or close to you.

You don't have to rehearse gestures, but you can plan on "showing" certain parts of the presentation as you go over your speech. Then your gestures should be natural and reinforcing to the message. Everyone is different in the size and amount of gestures used; you will appear conversational and natural by applying your own type of movement.

Clothing

The most important part is to choose clothes in which you feel comfortable. If you feel "different" or feel you have dressed inappropriately, you may not perform as well.

You probably want to dress similarly to the rest of the audience, make sure you ask about the dress code and then check again right before the event.

Do the clothes feel comfortable, or are they tight and restrictive? That means shoes, too. Are the clothes so flattering that they compete with you? Consider wearing something a little more subtle. Short skirts or tight trousers are out for presentations. Take everything out of your pockets. Do not carry lose change in your pockets.

Avoid wearing something new. You may find the clothes surprise you, tags you forgot to remove, ill fitting etc. The day before the speech, lay out all the clothes, shoes, you intend to wear so there are no last minute surprises, a stain on the tie, missing buttons. Avoid white socks and dark trousers. Men should wear long socks.

Red is often considered an emotional colour, and many experts don't recommend wearing it if the subject is controversial.

Avoid jewellery that is shiny, large, or dangling. Listeners tend to watch the movements and miss the message.

Consider your backdrop, too. A blue suit with a blue wall behind you may mean that you are lost in the background.

Voice

Good commentators who are known for excellent voice quality are trained, not born with that quality.

Practicing certain exercises will help you improve your voice and reach the natural sounds you were meant to have.

Volume, pitch and nasal problems can be solved often through better breathing habits. Breathing from the midsection, using the diaphragm and opening all air passage will fully help.

Other voice problems include speed, timing, change in pitch or volume, emphasis, accents, speech clarity including bad pronunciation and fillers such as "um", "em", "er", "like", "You know" etc. Most of these can be resolved with practice; the majority requires familiarity with the material. Remember, audiences like variation in pace. No monotones. So one of the most important things to remember is your tone and pace.

Practice reading different written materials out loud, newspaper articles, poetry etc. Use a recording device, record yourself reading a short paragraph, then listen and repeat the process at least a couple of times more, each time improving speed, emphasis, volume, pronunciation etc.

Pause! The power of pausing in a presentation can be very profound, but it must be practiced in the context of the message you want to deliver. It could come across badly, especially if you appear to continually pause, as it just looks like you have forgotten your speech. However, don't be afraid to pause after a question. Obviously thank the individual for the question and say something like, "good question" or "great question" then pause, this gives you time to accurately formulate a response to the question, but it will also give you a chance to catch your breath.

Foreign accents by the way are not problems, unless clear pronunciation is the issue. If you do have a foreign or regional accent, simply tell your audience where you were born so they don't miss your message while trying to guess your origin.

If you are speaking to an audience in a language that is not their first language, speak very carefully so that they will understand you.

Use language to suit the audience – familiar terms, relevant examples & illustrations.

If articulation is a problem, repeat all difficult words so that you are familiar with them. If some words give you problems, use alternatives.

Fillers can be helped by repeating the word or phrase every time you hear yourself say it, or by having someone else repeat it when they hear you say it. You'll find this repetition very frustrating, but it is worth it to eradicate those annoying fillers.

Avoid acronyms and abbreviations when possible.

Be optimistic, sound cheery and smile. Speak with passion and enthusiasm. If you speak passionately it will make up for many other shortcomings.

Notes

Decide: notes or no notes?

Use as few notes as possible, since the more you look at these, the less you look at your audience. Make reference to any notes as easy as possible, freeing you to maintain eye contact with your listeners.

There are two different types of notes: outlines and scripts. An outline provides you only with the major ideas you want to stress, summarizing your key points to keep you on track and ensure you don't miss anything. The script gives you the entire text of your speech. Obviously, brief notes allow for more spontaneity and eye contact, two major requirements for audience rapport. Excellent familiarity with a script is necessary to maintain the audience contact you need.

If writing notes, try using note cards instead of larger paper. Smaller cards are less visible and limit the amount you can put on each one, helping spontaneity. Make sure the type or print is large enough so that you can see it from where it will be placed as you are delivering the speech. Always print, no cursive/joined writing. Do not use type that has all capital letters as you are unaccustomed to reading this type and its unfamiliarity will make reading more difficult.

Number and clip all pages or cards, and keep your notes with you at all times.

Ensure that complete thoughts are not separated from page to page. Employ only the upper two-thirds of paper for writing if regular paper is used, eliminating having to drop your head so far down to the end of the sheet. Place notes in a cover or folder before walking to the lectern.

Before your speech, identify a place for your notes where they will be easily accessible to you. Place notes so that you have two unread cards/pages in front of you at all times. Look at the notes on the left, then slide the card/paper from the right to the left view, do not turn the page over, slide it.

Avoid holding the notes, but if you need to look at them more closely, pick them up when you use them, then replace them. When reading direct quotations, you can hold the note and read from the page.

If using a lectern, keep your hands on the lectern, not on the notes. Arrange for a space and a microphone that allows you to move away from the lectern when you can, then back to your notes when necessary. This movement helps keep you closer to the audience.

Don't write or change your notes just before you speak. You destroy the easy familiarity that having worked with them a few times in advance gives you.

Always keep a blank sheet and pen nearby before and during your presentation in case you need to note something.

Audience Engagement and Interaction

The secret to keeping your audience involved in your presentation is to keep them on ICE; you must Inform, Consider and Engage.

You may have to present detailed and technical information, without putting your audience to sleep. Presenting detailed information may be important but if your audience isn't engaged then the job of putting across this information is even harder.

Audience attention tends to falter in the middle of any speech or presentation, even a good one. If you want to maintain that attention, try some techniques that improve the quality and the interest level and can be used as attention grabbers.

Most people won't remember the ideas in your presentation as much as the concrete examples you use to illustrate those ideas or messages. Your examples help your audience understand and retain the ideas. Your stories and examples will make your speech come alive for your listeners, drawing vivid pictures to which they can relate. The more an audience can relate to examples, the more persuasive you will be. Look for examples that listeners will understand and illustrate your own objectives. Taking real life situations from the audience itself is useful too.

In presentations or speeches less really is more, no audience ever complained about a presentation or speech being too short.

Imagery
Using figurative language to create images in the listener's mind. Such as, describing a "conflagration" as a "fire the size of two and a half football fields"; market collapse, profits soaring etc.

Metaphors

Applying words or phrases symbolically, not literally, to indicate a comparison with the literal usage. "Food for thought," "Judgement day" and "Don't rock the boat" are metaphors.

Stories and Anecdotes

Citing stories or events to make points. Sales presentations often talk about satisfied customers as examples of how well a product or service works. Talk benefits, not features.

Current/Historical Events

Audiences especially like relating to what is happening in the news.

Exercises

Have the audience perform an exercise, let them experience your information all through the session. If the audience provides ideas or examples, use them, you supply the theory, in that way your information will be more convincing.

Humour

Not joke telling, just the funny or amusing side of life. Look for amusing stories. Self-humour is appreciated. The best funny anecdotes are the ones you tell about yourself, they seldom fail and the audience is usually on your side from then on.

Prizes and Surprises

Keep the audience guessing, "Before we finish, I will surprise you with some new information" or promise a prize later. Or just say something the audience doesn't expect.

Quotations

Quoting experts, your strategic plan, movies, songs, slogans are just a few of the possibilities. Quoting respectable people lends credibility and interest to your points. Be careful to quote people who are known and respected or this can work against you and that includes mispronunciation of the name of the person you quote.

Speaker Reference/Linking

Refer to other speaker's comments in your speech. Discussions during breaks can add value, letting you reference participant's names and ideas. Refer to people in the room or people they know.

Visuals

One of the most powerful things you can do to your presentation is to add in visual aids. Don't forget to give yourself plenty of time to prepare supporting visuals, and try to be creative – it doesn't always have to mean PowerPoint. Use visual aids where you can. This may include pictures, graphs, tables and or props. Some research shows that we only retain between 10% to 20% of what we hear. Visual reinforcement of key points, if used properly, however, can increase retention to between 60% or 70%. Other studies show that 80% of your audience will understand your message only if they see some visual reinforcement. It has also been assessed how we take in information during a presentation and indicators are that for text it is 7%, vocal is 38% with visual coming out on top at 55%. Ditch the bullet points, us pictures instead.

A picture speaks a thousand words....

Visuals are used to support, not to replace a good presentation. Presenters should not rely on the visuals, but should use them to enhance the speech. The prepared visual should be professional and supportive or it shouldn't be used at all.

Visuals should be introduced after the opening and introduction of your speech. You may compete with them during the most important parts of your presentation, the beginning and the end, if you use them then. Begin and close, with just you and the audience, unless you have a very special attention grabbing visual at these times.

Have the first visual ready to go, so that all you need to do when it is time, is turn it on. Audience retention rises when presented with a visual, so important points should be made at these times.

If using slides keep it short and simple (KISS), the audience can't listen to you and look at wordy information or slides at the same time. Show them only what you want them to see, when you want them to see it. Practice all visuals in advance. Position them onsite at the venue and check that everyone can see them. Remember, in handling audio visual equipment, anything that can go wrong, may go wrong. Prepare for any problems in advance, testing equipment, and locating backup or spare equipment. Better yet, be prepared to present with no visuals.

To point or not to point? That is the question. Experts disagree about using the pointer. Many recommend not using it at all, arguing that a well designed visual doesn't need it. While that is true, occasionally we may need to identify something specific on the screen.

Use pointers rarely, or only when you need to. For laser pointers, direct them slowly at what you want them to see on the screen; do not move the pointer very much.

Where do I look? Most audiences prefer that the presenter look at the large screen when introducing a visual. Doing so tells you immediately if the visual is properly placed. The big screen is a common point of reference, as well. After glancing at the visual, look back at the audience to discuss it, only looking quickly at the screen when necessary. Don't let the screen become your audience. Your eye contact should be with the audience 80%-90% and the screen 10%- 20% of the time.

Be careful to turn off the visual when not in use since its visibility is distracting to the audience. You want to draw attention back to you between visuals, so blank the screen to gain full attention as you speak. Whatever you use, avoid a big, brightly lit screen with no visual on it and avoid having a projected visual that is no longer relevant to your words.

For bullet points with power point, use animations so that the one you are talking about appears when you need it and not before.

Props and Demonstrations
Bring an item to show. Hide it until you are ready to show it, hold it up so that all can see, then put it away, out of sight.

5 MANAGE STAGE FRIGHT

Lose the fear, get out there and speak! In virtually every case, a person's fear of public speaking is unjustified. What is the worst that could happen? You could trip on stage, freeze, forget a sentence, fumble a line, stammer or shake. None of these are fatal. The worst that could happen probably won't, and even if it does, you will live through it. But still the fear of public speaking is considered by many as their number one fear, above even the fear of death, disease or divorce.

If you feel uncomfortable at even the thought of giving presentations or speaking in public, don't worry, anxiety is a normal response for anyone whose actions are open to such public scrutiny. Fortunately for most speakers, the audience cannot detect your internal discomfort. You may feel it, but they cannot see it. That anxiety may even prevent us from reaching our fullest potential since we may tend to avoid speaking opportunities altogether that could help advance our career.

Stage fright is a result of the "fight or flight" response dictated by the most primitive part of the brain. Stage fright is adrenaline, extra energy, which can actually improve your presentation or speech, if you harness it and use it properly. Learn to control that extra energy and make it work for you.

While there are many effective methods of relaxation that can help reduce our fear of public speaking, the most important step is fundamental. We must begin by recognizing that making presentations and public speaking is a skill and must be learned. It is not something we can simply get up and do effectively without basic training and practice. The most important thing you can do to alleviate sweaty palms is to practice, practice, practice.

Many people learn to make presentations in front of relatively small groups of people.

When it comes to presenting yourself, your ideas or your business to an audience of hundreds at a conference, panic can easily set in. But it all comes down to preparation and practice, practice, practice. The size of the audience should have no bearing on your performance. Whether you are presenting to one or one thousand your approach and delivery should be exactly the same.

These suggestions will help alleviate stage fright and enhance your delivery:

- **Prepare** – A well prepared speaker isn't nearly as nervous as a poorly prepared one.

- **Breathe** – As you are waiting to speak, breathe deeply.

- **Meet and Greet** – Observe your audience as they arrive, personally introduce yourself to members of the audience, shake hands, exchange pleasantries, ask questions.

- **Listen and Link** – Listen to the speaker before you and your introduction carefully. Make a link, as this will help you focus on the event and the message you want to deliver.

- **Take a moment** – Before beginning, arrange your notes and catch your breath.

- **Visualize** – Before you speak, envision yourself completing the presentation successfully. You'll find your vision is likely to come through.

- **Opening** – Start by linking to the previous speaker and then commence with your own presentation.

- **Avoid**

  - Speaking rapidly at the beginning or worse yet, begin before even reaching the stage.

  - Using a pointer or instrument if you tend to be uneasy during the beginning as it may betray a shaky hand. If you do use a pointer or instrument do not continue holding it after you have used it.

  - Picking up a glass of water or anything else so that your hands may give you away.

  - Dairy products and cold/carbonated beverages.

  - Holding on to the lectern. Do not put your hands in your pockets.

6 DIFFICULT AUDIENCE/QUESTIONS

Remember most audiences want your presentation to go well. They want to engage you. But, in nearly every audience there will be one person who you feel loathes you on sight. Can't stand your voice, hates your clothes, and assumes you're stupid. Usually they are in the front row glaring at you. IGNORE them. You cannot win this person over, no matter how well you speak. Yes, it is difficult and unpleasant to feel those negative stares coming your way but your job is to work with the rest of the audience, who are ready to listen to you. If you focus too hard on negative glarer you will try too hard, confuse and lose the remainder of your audience. Most of these negative glarer's just want to leave the room as soon as possible, not interested in questions, in fact they don't even want to be there in the first place.

If negative glarer does ask a hostile or difficult question, make sure you listen, and be ready to gently ask them a question, to expand, provide more information to ensure you understand the question properly. This also gives you time to assess if they are truly hostile and of course to accurately formulate a response to the question. Never ever respond defensively or aggressively, even if you are right, the whole audience will resent you for the tone of your response, picking on the questioner. The audience will become closed and it is unlikely you will receive further questions, not a good way to end what otherwise may have been an excellent presentation.

So with questions, difficult or not, listen respectfully, don't make personal attacks, say what you mean and mean what you say. Do not interrupt people when they are speaking. In the face of difficult or hostile questioning where appropriate you can invite comments from the audience, make it an open discussion.

Don't be afraid to state what is obvious to you, it may not be obvious to the audience. Also remember if there is a question you cannot answer, take the question away so as to provide more information and a complete and accurate response, make sure you get the contact details of the questioner and then do what you promised and provide a timely response to their question. If you have attempted to answer a question and 'you get into a hole', stop digging! In other words, if things start to go badly when answering a question, stop, don't make things worse, calmly advise that you need to investigate further and take the question away to provide a response later.

And actually, if you get a negative glarer in your audience, you know sometimes they turn out to be short sighted and hard of hearing, sitting in the front and frowning terrible in their effort to listen to you. Genuinely nice, decent individuals.

ABOUT THE AUTHOR

With over seventeen years experience in the Payments industry, Stephen has extensive experience of business and IT related change programmes, with a strong planning and management ethos. Stephen is extremely dedicated and professional and strong in many areas from analysis to customer presentations and his attention to detail ensures his delivery is consistently of a very high standard. He demonstrates thought leadership and knows what actions to take in challenging situations, with a heavy focus on the customer to ensure superior levels of service and satisfaction. Stephen has worked and spoken internationally for a number of years. He currently works and resides in Ireland with his wife and two young daughters.

11521190R00025

Printed in Germany
by Amazon Distribution
GmbH, Leipzig